NEW ZEALAND

R.L. Van

Big Buddy Books
An Imprint of Abdo Publishing
abdobooks.com

abdobooks.com

Published by Abdo Publishing, a division of ABDO, PO Box 398166, Minneapolis, Minnesota 55439. Copyright © 2023 by Abdo Consulting Group, Inc. International copyrights reserved in all countries. No part of this book may be reproduced in any form without written permission from the publisher. Big Buddy Books™ is a trademark and logo of Abdo Publishing.

Printed in the United States of America, North Mankato, Minnesota
102022
012023

Design: Emily O'Malley, Mighty Media, Inc.
Production: Mighty Media, Inc.
Editor: Jessica Rusick
Cover Photograph: Nikolay 007/Shutterstock Images
Interior Photographs: Archives New Zealand/Wikimedia Commons, p. 28 (bottom); AsiaTravel/Shutterstock Images, p. 26 (right); ChameleonsEye/Shutterstock Images, p. 13; Colin McDiarmid/Wikimedia Commons, p. 29 (bottom left); Darrenp/Shutterstock Images, p. 29 (top); DFree/Shutterstock Images, p. 21; Dmitry Naumov/Shutterstock Images, p. 6 (bottom); eddyrick/Shutterstock Images, p. 30 (flag); Ekaterina Markelova/Shutterstock Images, p. 19; Everett Collection/Shutterstock Images, p. 28 (top left); Filip Bjorkman/Shutterstock Images, p. 7 (map); Jiri Foltyn/Shutterstock Images, p. 27 (bottom); Klanarong Chitmung/Shutterstock Images, p. 27 (top right); lukulo/iStockphoto, pp. 5 (compass), 7 (compass); Mark Schwettmann/Shutterstock Images, p. 15; Martin M303/Shutterstock Images, p. 25; munalin/Shutterstock Images, p. 30 (currency); New Zealand Government Office of the Governor General/Wikimedia Commons, p. 29 (bottom right); Nikolay 007/Shutterstock Images, p. 27 (top left); Paul Looyen/Shutterstock Images, p. 17; Phil Nobel/AP Images, p. 26 (left); Pyty/Shutterstock Images, p. 5 (map); Robert CHG/Shutterstock Images, p. 6 (top); Stargrass/Shutterstock Images, p. 6 (middle); Tinseltown/Shutterstock Images, p. 23; trabantos/Shutterstock Images, p. 28 (top right); W Bulach/Wikimedia Commons, p. 9; Yevgen Belich/Shutterstock Images, p. 11
Design Elements: Mighty Media, Inc.
Country population and area figures taken from the CIA World Factbook

Library of Congress Control Number: 2022940503

Publisher's Cataloging-in-Publication Data
Names: Van, R.L., author.
Title: New Zealand / by R.L. Van
Description: Minneapolis, Minnesota : Abdo Publishing, 2023 | Series: Countries | Includes online resources and index.
Identifiers: ISBN 9781532199691 (lib. bdg.) | ISBN 9781098274894 (ebook)
Subjects: LCSH: New Zealand--Juvenile literature. | Islands of the Pacific--Juvenile literature. | New Zealand--History--Juvenile literature. | Geography--Juvenile literature.
Classification: DDC 993--dc23

CONTENTS

Passport to New Zealand..4

Important Cities..6

New Zealand in History..8

An Important Symbol..12

Across the Land..14

Earning a Living..16

Life in New Zealand..18

Famous Faces..20

A Great Country..24

Tour Book..26

Timeline..28

New Zealand Up Close..30

Glossary..31

Online Resources..31

Index..32

PASSPORT TO NEW ZEALAND

New Zealand is a country in the Pacific Ocean. It is made up of more than 600 islands. The two main islands are the North Island and the South Island. More than 5 million people live in New Zealand.

WHERE IS NEW ZEALAND?

NEW ZEALAND

North Island

South Island

Tasman Sea

Pacific Ocean

IMPORTANT CITIES

Wellington is New Zealand's **capital** and second-largest city. It is known for its food and culture.

Auckland is New Zealand's largest city. It is a diverse city and a center of business and culture.

Christchurch is New Zealand's third-largest city. It is known for the arts and its many parks.

Auckland
Population: 1.65 million

NEW ZEALAND

Wellington
Population: 419,000

Christchurch
Population: 363,926

DID YOU KNOW?

Auckland has two harbors and is nicknamed the "City of Sails."

SAY IT

Wellington
WEH-ling-tuhn

Auckland
AWK-lend

Christchurch
CRYST-cherch

7

NEW ZEALAND IN HISTORY

People arrived in what is now New Zealand in the 1200s. They were the **ancestors** of the native Māori people. In the 1700s, Europeans came to the area to trade goods. Over time, Europeans took Māori land and changed their way of life.

SAY IT

Māori
MAU-ree

Ancient peoples came to New Zealand in large seafaring canoes.

In 1840, New Zealand became a British colony. Twelve years later, the Constitution Act created New Zealand's government. There were many conflicts between the Māori and settlers. It took years to bring peace. In 1947, New Zealand became a fully independent nation.

Facial tattoos are sacred in Māori culture. Some modern Māori choose to wear them.

AN IMPORTANT SYMBOL

New Zealand's flag is red and blue. It includes the United Kingdom flag. New Zealand is a **federal parliamentary democracy**. Parliament makes laws. The prime minister leads government. A governor-general represents the United Kingdom's king or queen.

The stars on New Zealand's flag represent the Southern Cross constellation.

ACROSS THE LAND

New Zealand is known for its beautiful land. It has **fjords**, mountains, **volcanoes**, forests, **glaciers**, and farmland.

Skinks, geckos, bats, fish, and flightless birds live in New Zealand. Ferns, liverworts, and gorse grow there.

SAY IT

fjord
FYORD

All of New Zealand's fjords are on South Island.

EARNING A LIVING

Factory workers in New Zealand make food products, machines, and paper. Most people have service jobs, such as banking.

New Zealand's **natural resources** include coal, gold, and timber. Farmers grow apples, barley, and kiwifruit. They raise cattle and sheep.

Milk is one of New Zealand's main exports.

LIFE IN NEW ZEALAND

New Zealand's popular foods include beef, seafood, and a dessert called pavlova. New Zealanders enjoy watching rugby, cricket, and netball. Many people enjoy hiking, boating, and skiing.

DID YOU KNOW?

New Zealand's rugby team is called the All Blacks.

Pavlova is made of whipped egg whites. It has a crisp outside and soft inside.

FAMOUS FACES

Taika Waititi grew up in Raukokore and Wellington. He writes, directs, and acts in movies and TV shows. Waititi is known for his work on *Thor* movies and *Star Wars* projects. In 2020, he became the first Māori to win an Academy Award for adapted screenplay.

SAY IT

Taika Waititi
TIE-kuh WHY-tee-tee

Taika Waititi has directed two *Thor* movies. He also voices the character Korg!

Lorde was born and raised near Auckland. She began singing at a young age. In 2012, her song "Royals" brought her international attention. Lorde has since sold millions of albums. She has also won two Grammy Awards. She is considered a unique, influential artist.

Lorde's given name is Ella Marija Lani Yelich-O'Connor.

A GREAT COUNTRY

New Zealand has beautiful land and a unique history and culture. The people and places of New Zealand help make the world a more interesting place.

Tongariro is New Zealand's oldest national park. It has volcanoes, emerald lakes, and Māori religious sites.

TOUR BOOK

If you ever visit New Zealand, here are some places to go and things to do!

SEE

Learn about New Zealand's famous kiwi birds at the National Kiwi Hatchery in Rotorua.

LEARN

Take a tour of New Zealand's national museum, Te Papa, in Wellington.

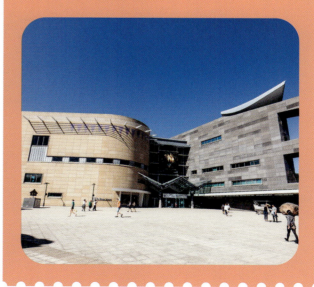

DISCOVER

The *Lord of the Rings* movies were filmed in New Zealand. Explore the Shire at the Hobbiton Movie Set!

EXPLORE

Take a boat ride on the underground river through the Waitomo Caves. They are filled with glow worms!

CLIMB

See New Zealand from the top of Auckland's Sky Tower, the tallest freestanding structure in the southern **hemisphere**.

TIMELINE

1769
James Cook arrived in New Zealand and began mapping the islands.

1893
New Zealand became the first country to give women the right to vote.

1840
The British and Māori signed the Treaty of Waitangi, giving ruling power of New Zealand to the queen of England.

1908
Native New Zealander Ernest Rutherford received a Nobel Prize in Chemistry.

1947
New Zealand became fully independent.

2011
While Christchurch was still recovering from a 2010 **earthquake**, another major earthquake struck the city. More than 180 people were killed.

1997
Jenny Shipley became New Zealand's first woman prime minister.

2021
Dame Cindy Kiro became New Zealand's first Māori governor-general.

NEW ZEALAND
UP CLOSE

Official Name
New Zealand
("Aotearoa" in Māori)

Flag

Population
5,053,004 (2022 est.)
125th-most-populated country

Total Area
103,799 square miles
(268,838 sq km)
76th-largest country

Official Languages
English, Māori, New
Zealand Sign Language

Capital
Wellington

Currency
New Zealand dollar

National Anthem
"God Defend
New Zealand"

Form of Government
Federal parliamentary
democracy under
a constitutional
monarchy

GLOSSARY

ancestors—family members from an earlier time.

capital—a city where government leaders meet.

earthquake (UHRTH-kwayk)—a shaking of a part of the earth.

federal parliamentary democracy—a government in which people elect representatives to parliament, and these representatives choose a leader. The central government and the individual states and territories share power.

fjord—a narrow section of ocean reaching into the land between two high cliffs.

glacier (GLAY-shuhr)—a huge chunk of ice and snow on land.

hemisphere (HEH-muhs-feer)—one half of Earth.

natural resources—useful and valuable supplies from nature.

volcano—a deep opening in Earth's surface from which hot liquid rock or steam comes out.

ONLINE RESOURCES

To learn more about New Zealand, please visit **abdobooklinks.com** or scan this QR code. These links are routinely monitored and updated to provide the most current information available.

INDEX

animals, 14, 16, 26, 27

Auckland, 6, 7, 22, 27

businesses, 6, 16

Christchurch, 6, 7, 29

Cook, James, 28

flag, 12, 13, 30

food, 6, 16, 18, 19

government, 10, 12, 28, 29, 30

Hobbiton Movie Set, 27

Kiro, Dame Cindy, 29

language, 30

Lorde, 22, 23

Māori, 8, 10, 11, 20, 25, 28, 29, 30

National Kiwi Hatchery, 26

natural resources, 16, 17

North Island, 4, 5

Pacific Ocean, 4, 5

plants, 14, 16

population, 4, 7, 30

Rutherford, Ernest, 28

Shipley, Jenny, 29

size, 30

South Island, 4, 5, 15

sports, 18

Te Papa, 26

Tongariro, 25

Treaty of Waitangi, 28

United Kingdom, 10, 12, 28

Waititi, Taika, 20, 21

Waitomo Caves, 27

Wellington, 6, 7, 20, 26, 30